DATE DUE

"Boy Walking Bottom of Pool," 1981 by

Laurie Simmons
Courtesy of the artist and
Sperone Westwater Gallery

Author photo by

Thomas H. Garver

Published in the United States by

Fence Books
303 East Eighth Street, #B1
New York, NY 10009
www.fencebooks.com

Book design by

Rebecca Wolff

Fence Books are distributed by

University Press of New England
www.upne.com

and printed in Canada by

Westcan Printing Group
www.westcanpg.com

Library of Congress Cataloguing in Publication Data
        Sims, Laura [1973–]
        Practice, Restraint / Laura Sims

Library of Congress Control Number: 2005933980

ISBN 0-9740909-9-9

FIRST EDITION

Many thanks to

My family—by nature, nurture, and marriage.

My friends, who are family.

My writer-friends in Madison, Milwaukee, Chicago, New York, and elsewhere—my community.

My teachers—with special thanks to Henry Hart, Bonnie Martin, Nancy Schoenberger, and Paige Whitten.

My students at Madison Area Technical College.

My co-workers at Home Savings Bank.

The editors of the following journals and web sites where many of these poems appeared: *Bird Dog, Columbia Poetry Review, Conduit, Esther Press, Fence, First Intensity, Gam, Good Foot, How2, Indiana Review, jubilat, La Petite Zine, LIT, Nedge, Northwest Review, 6x6, 3rd Bed,* and *26*.

The section "Bank Book" is dedicated to Margaret Lewis, and to the memory of our mothers, Anne Teefey and Ann McDuff.

The first fourteen poems from the section "Bank Book" were originally printed as a limited-edition chapbook by Answer Tag Press, which also printed a broadside of "Suffering Succotash." The section "Paperback Book" first appeared as a chapbook in *3rd Bed*. David Pavelich, Editor of Answer Tag Press, and Vincent Standley, Hermine Meinhard, and Andrea Baker, editors of *3rd Bed,* have been extremely supportive of my work, and I thank them.

I would also like to thank the artist Bodo Korsig for making a limited-edition accordion book of the poem "Winter in You."

Last but certainly not least, I would like to thank the Alberta DuPont Bonsal Foundation, Tom Thompson, and Rebecca Wolff for their generous support.

LAURA SIMS

Practice, Restraint

For Corey, first and foremost

Contents

I. Lost Book

"Winter in You"   1

Your Second Head   3

Platitude   5

Lyrical Plot, with Ephemera   7

Resurrection, Parade   10

Ruth   11

Former Relation   13

Spin   15

Little House   16

II. Bank Book

BANK ONE – BANK THIRTY-THREE   21 – 59

III. Work Book

Hourly/Daily   63

Public Works   64

Moses   67

Work   68

IV. War Book

Africa   73

Homage   75

Suffering Succotash   77

Musical, Chemical, Figurine   78

Democracy   80

V. Paperback Book

Lake   85

Former Quarry Song   86

Eternity vs. The Throttler   88

Restaurants, The Howling Alley, Fields   89

"Hold Me Closer than That"   91

Locust v. Anchorite   94

Paperback   96

Poem   98

I. Lost Book

"Winter in You"

Have I seen such a tower

Her fleshy, spectacular hand

Would the dogs not find

A tower of ash when the hearth wound down

What it costs

to put winter in you!

Her nails cleanly sculpted, bare

And the autumn?

One buys tires for life

Ablaze—

Then her hair falls down

Her hand

Is the winter

lost, little innocent people?

Your Second Head

Fell longingly

Into place

Christ—

Those brambles

Swept from the forehead

All leafiness, silence

Where harmony, love & delusion

A basket

Was it kingly of them

Their foaming cups

Their hands at the crisp

Folded edge of an invoice

Platitude

nowhere and nowhere concerned

with your welfare,

albeit a strange one

The doll looks on.

With a plush human face

the fowl looks on.

Wings over water anticipate

landing

In threes, by the porcelain toes

Underwater.

This is the glassed-in city,

these are its gates.

This tiny hand

is the gatekeeper's wife

in a gesture of solace

unlikely, unlikely,

the sound of her voice

Lyrical Plot, with Ephemera

All at once on the Sumida River—

a planet   or basket

conveniently placed

strolling the riverbank,
folk

                    wearing hats
                    under parasols

rice-paper skin

                    for all of eternity,
                    here is my beauty

The earthquake raises them up

and rejects them. Raises them up

and rejects them.

Bold repetition,

a craving for story necessitates

plot

        on the part
        of the gentlemen bankers
        in hats

        their wives in kimono
        or Western confection

taking air—

legs v-ed up in the air

their backs riding air

fingers apart

        their hair falling out
        of the complex plot

the hairpins

the ornaments, varied

Resurrection, Parade

Elaborate, this metalwork grille on the church face.

These cross-marked trees.

This way to the water tank.

Tinny notes played by a chimp.

Something worse.

What images come to mind!

The organ instructing—

Head for the swell, hang a right.

Her long black braid.

As I write you, dearest, I find two stairways spiraling up.

She turns at the waist

Wearing pearl-gray gloves

A blur.

Immeasurable, these heady notes.

Ruth

what good is she then
wearing lightweight combs

in her hair in the v-shaped
valley, then far

from the v-shaped valley
on fire: the field

plus everything wood

in the world
what glorified branch reads

"one limb lost from another"
among the tall grasses

the prairie distracts her

from bellowing Mary
whose bloodlines Ruth

has eschewed for some
twenty-nine years

in the storm shack
pulling her hair down

afraid

not the thought
of her drowning in that

but the other, that peerless contraption

Former Relation

A basement, a valley—

the flayed earth is something to see.

*

What do you hail when hailing me? A pillow.

A soft white pillow at dusk.

*

The answer has twisted its mouth

*

Filling the room with a lovely condition

forever, your wife, at the cold

sundial.

*

A climber of sorts

in the window, the cosmos

*

as Jacob, not Anne. When I hailed you

as Anne

in the tunnel, hands

Spin

This is life on a cooling planet,

I guess,

Marguerite says. Help me,

I'm shaking.

She sings of star-crossed lovers

horizontally stacked in the past, herself

being one of a set. Help me,

it hurts. She says it is burning

but pleasant.

The crowd cries back:

This is life on a cooling planet,

I guess. If it has no soul

then it has no soul.

Little House

Mother's smooth, parted hair

Hands busy with light

The buttons that buttoned her basque up the front

And the girls – little waists
Under wings of sleek hair

*

A bright new bullet
Shiny new bullets
Their shining eyes

*

Wearing only a loincloth

He curried the horses

*

Till all the meat fell from the bones

*

(Now

It can never be long, long ago

II. Bank Book

for Margaret

BANK ONE

She sought an escape goat

To ride in and out of the vault

Bearing gold bars

Into the desert

Where snakes would have her

Is it my mother

She wondered aloud

Stroking the cold slippery surface

Of purest form

Through the canvas bag

BANK TWO

The tragedy's lapse: was she

Fat

We wonder

Counting on

So many tickets in stock

Be they yellow

The blue of withdrawal

With our eyes shut

She seems

Nearly verdant

Nearly our family tree

Standing under our regular

Lover

BANK THREE

I am new

I left my dress

In the film

A body of water

BANK FOUR

For David Markson

She resigns

One-armed

To a place of contempt

Wearing nettles all over

The sea

Her vanished arm

Makes a point—

Snubbing her daily

BANK FIVE

She gave back

The marble view

With picnics, dome

*

The long, green lawn

*

Everything she's worked for

Everything slaved

Everything she's sold her children

To Carthage—

waving her arms

*

The fools

Whose tools of writing

Are savage / Are these?

BANK SIX

If you climb on now

What penance

Requires

One girl

Down in the marsh

Not for that

Not for all the cold cash in the world would I do it

But one man

Yes

Resolves the particulars

Later

BANK SEVEN

Tit for tat

Your border *gives in*

      Under the wet awning, a bomb

Or something

We think—

      We were animals

Friend

BANK EIGHT

A light

Drowning, sculpture—

    It's small enough

    Isn't she small enough

    Down at the branch level / lake floor:

    Soapstone, euphoria, coin?

BANK NINE

"As our mothers would tell us, if they could speak."
—Anon., 18th c.

What took her

I'd tell her

The blink of an eye

The long stretch, with poppies

The lie "without you"

I'd tell her

What took her

Deflects itself

Silly—

The clown will live

BANK TEN

This happens to be

Time

Out of mind

In a t-shirt

Reclining by water

Our spotless—

Our eyes

Have seen sandier shores and whiter

When cancer

Ran in the family

BANK ELEVEN

See

How easy it is

Horned

And dissembling

What price is this

A price

At all?

BANK TWELVE

Half-baked

The children running toward light

I polished the bricks

In those moments

My house was shining

BANK THIRTEEN

Her child in a monkey's

Superior arms

Over: forest, wetlands, prairie, savanna, and falls

*

For six hours

Beyond

This sitting position

BANK FOURTEEN

Branding a world

In which daisies

Appear as if

You who were

The yard lady

Turn

In the parking garage

Your logo

Bearing you

Gravely

BANK FIFTEEN

In every backyard

A peacock

Or some green nonsense

Refuting

What rifles report from her far-flung states

BANK SIXTEEN

The pills have grown

Trees

Let this year be a year

Of presents

To the weird authentic

Let's speak with one voice

To a brassy red

On an 'ugly sea'

Rank

And redundant

Dwindles away

'Into native element'

Money

Aren't you a bird

BANK SEVENTEEN

At the east branch—

One empty room

And another

Abandoned

By Spaniards

BANK EIGHTEEN

Dear

It left its

Permanent handprint

On you

Which is what the world

Eating magazines

Grins

BANK NINETEEN

My water weight

Shifts

To include

What the horde assumes—

A fully sown field, a bun in

Nothing

Conceived of

(Land)

BANK TWENTY

No more moving between

Crummy sets

Work – bar – house – table – bed

No more putting off

Later what others

Can do to you now

Look down

Revolves Around Prostitute's Head

You

Who

Someone

& End

BANK TWENTY-ONE

Your future starts here

In a state of arousal

Doesn't it

Hurt

When they turn

Fifty-nine

And a half

BANK TWENTY-TWO

The infinite

Network of rooms

*

When

Nobody wants you enough

BANK TWENTY-THREE

I held my child

Under the cup

Of kings

In a valley

Where one great pyramid

Rose

In a jungle weave

I'm sure of it—

Here is a chamber

In which

She came to

BANK TWENTY-FOUR

It's no longer about singing

I can't stand

When you sing

About the way her done-in face—

And the world

For a moment

I felt

I can't stand when you sing

BANK TWENTY-FIVE

It's something—

Your body, my car

Laid down in the tunnel of noise

For a reason

The white

Half-

Hour

BANK TWENTY-SIX

Why you are

Borrowed from

Time

The flat land flattens more

Or

The desert heft

Of the conference room

*

You're included

For someone's

Unknowing

And yours

A cloud whose bounty is

Where you are

BANK TWENTY-SEVEN

A wave fixes

The world

One

Playscape

By one

*

Not here—

        (Off-screen: mammalian

*

My place

Agony

Yours

Is permanent

Man

BANK TWENTY-EIGHT

Tree

How is Paris

(I know)

To the rest of you lodged in my mind

I'm a hamster

On a train from the war

En route from the war

Honestly

Why does it all have to lead

To these reins—

I will go

BANK TWENTY-NINE

What room

What anchored space

Where what

Machine

From time before time

Emptied

What man

In the middle of

What

Draperies

BANK THIRTY

What is

Money

Is colorful

Under her hand

Is a basket

Of fruit she carries

Shoreward

She longs for

Far

From her country

BANK THIRTY-ONE

Trees over here

Over there

In one empty classroom

The girl is turning

The town inside out

*

The worst is

Belonging

BANK THIRTY-TWO

Both of us opened

In windows / en face de

Who froze   in the field

Between   road and wood

What's yours

Settles mine, my mind—

There's a staircase facing the porch door, patio, sea, you are

Right

BANK THIRTY-THREE

There were balustrades

There

And water filming the smooth interior wall

Time for coloring in

(A gown, a car)

There you sit in a room

Subdued

III. Work Book

Hourly / Daily

The legwork done

By lesser organs of the afternoon

Lies hard on the world

Where are organs permitted

Conditions like this?

Is there someone

Committing the city? Someone in plaid

Drew a knife from the ham saying, "this one"

The organs command, my father has done it

Again when a man

Sulks down the aisle

Making cake, and lush greenery

Public Works

Those pre-hung doors

of the native state / the return

to a native, pre-eminent state

wholly immanent, wise

and woolly.

What will be permanent matters

to calming devices

      the whims of an ice age

Where others have failed do you think this hump

addled by chicanes, chokers,

narrowings, neck downs

      This is life on a median island, I guess.

One makes up a host

of confinements by which to abide, in a galaxy

armed with a featherweight touch—

only joking

Moses

Fourteen lanes

with sky on one end

and the end

of the human disgrace

on the other—

a fetish, the urban form

a lake

is self-regard but a highway

slithers

the car

grows skin after skin on its errand from God

If you finish your supper,

from one end of this mess to the other,

rewards

Work

I.

We will all wear shirts bearing "staff."

Michelle will buy silvery hats.

A whistling in trees.

II.

the long ride bleeding her

Now she gives up; we berate her

(If you are not well, you will not be left alone.)

for something she's lost in the water, her hat

on the head of a sea chicken

III.

The great city waits for an echoing crack

a signal for "party."

"Their love for each other is comely,"

collecting the teacups

IV.

It was diction alone, and a curious rhythm. What, after
all, was the ride to the island?

One in one egg, one in another. Michelle's thoughts

drift to the water below. In the trees, she was godly.
Back then, her silvery hat

On the water

She thought

IV. War Book

Africa

In mercy a notion of the finished form

like others before them

      in rabbit holes

What was that ruckus in the other room?

When you tire

the stone bottle placed on a dune—

      milk at dawn

      religion at lamplight

Inside it's a furnace. The boys drink Turkish tea

straight from her lips. Gaily dressed,

this block

resembles my back yard

in Africa.

Homage

In the fog of war, Edgar finds

his hands and knees

have turned. From a comely violet

to mauve, the sky and Anna's dress

revolve in hell

around a mirrored globe.

Edgar, "we are feckless, cheap,

and have the attention spans of fleas."

His mother gasps politely

in the drawing room; the bride

must fathom Edgar

leaning on his bridal statuette.

"The economy is down, we're on our knees,

our sunny dispositions falter."

Befuddled, wed, somewhere

in the desert, Edgar turns

a fulsome breath upon his country, names it

Honey.

Suffering Succotash

All dead men

In the mercury dusk of spring

In particular

Those who were felled

In one patch of highway scrub brush & trees

This regime, or a _____ one

We have never been happier

Shedding our clothes than we were

That evening you mention. The silty light

And it flattened our skin tone and hair.

Musical, Chemical, Figurine

In cut-offs, wearing a necklace of coral—

the dead from the mountain.

Suddenness raises this dust in the air.

    "I moved a mountain and men came out"

    "and also made rounds of the hotel lobby"

    "looked up to see beds in the sky"

    "in formation, both women and men, disheveled"

    "but calmly descending"

    "a smell in the air"

    "of chlorine—the kidney-shaped pool"

filled with ice cubes. Filled with perfection

Honored

with wire

and stars,

the dead,

held aloft,

on a velvety couch in the lobby: a damp spot,

whose suddenness

opens the way

Democracy

One verdant minute

after the next, the love of the people

eludes him.

What does it mean? One thing unfolds

as a chain of things: the failure of making

a fantasy park

out of war

in an armchair,

the passage of hundreds of years

the loss of perpetual motion, the line

that proceeds

"a dark sky, and nothing but fire"

in his absence, the absence

of millions

V. Paperback Book

Lake

"Girl Walks Home Over Water"

Under whose gaze, in what desert, etc.

*

She is glistening plain.

Lovely, returning her dead

In the spotless car

Former Quarry Song

Let her tell me in the ear they are almost you.

Let them kill her in the quarry. The tissue

And stuff wadded up in the tissue are white,

Yet he snags me with color. The colors

Themselves when you call. Let her

Hair fall out in the water, let her stir up

Terrible peanuts of noise. Broke on the rock.

First, the everyday diction appearing

To dive. She looks up at the vacant lot

From her body's stirring resemblance.

And the road beyond sings tauntingly

Fondly of love. Let one bird whistle

And one bird cough in response. She bungles her

Crime / flips like a fish / flashes her belly.

Up at em. Hallowed the breath of the lake.

Tell me deep in the ear when you do, there

Is even a physical likeness. Trees arched

Over to see her. To see it. To see them leave

Through myriad fortress doors. Bright white

Cotton arming a pair of buzzards, like you.

Eternity vs. The Throttler

Blue discs laid in the grass

*

I learned to do this with my hands

*
*

At noon I mopped blood

In the back where they keep MSG

*

And untied her machine

*

At the water

*

I slipped

And used an "I love you"

Pnigalion,

bringer of light.

Restaurants, The Howling Alley, Fields

A surplus of something

like corn.

The corn in this region,

known for its puerile

condition, and bite marks

taking a girl by surprise.

Or noise,
a surplus of noise.

'The one you have wanted

is nobody living'

claiming a shoulder;

the left or the right?

The left: also known

as the sinister spot,

bargained from red.

Do you know

I've told you time

and again how thin she is,

Mister. 'Farms

and the corn took over

again.'

"Hold Me Closer than That"

We grew up among gross noises

in the global city,

incorporated as moss,

a moss-covered spot,

something inert

and slyly musical in the transplanted bamboo grove

sallied forth among systems,

hybrid and otherwise

raised pigment from sand,

revealed ourselves as a flash of white shirt

at the edge of the candlelit revel,

as you who mark yourselves with hiccoughs and sex

hiccough,

navigate Thebes.

We let in the wolves

wearing white shirts over their hair,

the word "hirsute"

culled from its dazzling height,

the myth from its canopied bedroom

---

saw the small beauty queen

on her deathbed

or bathtub,

candied in permanent drag

---

pared the nails of the parers who wielded tape

---

for the closing of mouths,

we wore her stars and stripes to the outside of parties,

heeding those who heeded words,

clearly

---

as you hailed these marks

we healed the skin around the sutures.

She was inappropriately young.

At the who's-who birthday party

courting doom

into youth

and back out,

she flicked her lids and followed us

to the fountain's center

where a bed-shaped island

lay buried under sand

at great cost to the city's makers.

Locust v. Anchorite

Who chose the locust to run aground

Why did it go out to sea

To come back bottled

Raging for leisure

Our prize

See us scatter our cards

The locust rears up

Stains the linoleum faintly

Let it strand itself on the beach

Let it let down its hair

Let it crawl right up to our hut

With its spiral of smoke

And acquire a level of comfort

We will bury it

No one but no one believes

And nothing but trouble

Will come

Of its stay in this homespun concoction

This paradise

One can exist

Neither more nor less

There is neither a ship nor room in the universe

Simply

Paperback

so many

dead girls

in this shit-hole

cave,

Batman,

says Robin,

his ward

left in charge

of the lot

of their streamlined

monotonous

fairy-tale

island-whore

getaways

Poem

This is the park where flowers were fitted in spaces and fed.

I myself have been grimacing back.

Comprenez-vous? I offer to pencil you into my Book on Color.

This is the park where trees hang under the lake.

What did I offer you then? A vial of red? A little pressed boy in a cap?

Pencilled myself into beauty.

This is the park where Gladhands rummaged the lake.

Back into girlhood. How would you know him?

I myself have nicknamed the fountain's shades: Pumpkin, Honey-Bun,
Witness, Sorry, and Sloth.

Do you remember him dying into the lake? He came up littered and silly.

Look for your name under "Table of Colors."

This is the park where

This is the park beauty
hangs in the lake and the needle-pines point

You will be featured on page 35 under "Salmon Pink."

back into beauty, girlhood, his cap. He was small and fit snugly into the dive.

Fence Books is an extension of **FENCE**, a biannual journal of poetry, fiction, art, and criticism that has a mission to redefine the terms of accessibility by publishing challenging writing distinguished by idiosyncrasy and intelligence rather than by allegiance with camps, schools, or cliques. It is part of our press's mission to support writers who might otherwise have difficulty being recognized because their work doesn't answer to either the mainstream or to recognizable modes of experimentation.

The Alberta Prize is an annual series administered by Fence Books in collaboration with the Alberta duPont Bonsal Foundation. The Alberta Prize offers publication of a first or second book of poems by a woman, as well as a five thousand dollar cash prize.

Our second prize series is the **Fence Modern Poets Series.** This contest is open to poets of either gender and at any stage of career, and offers a one thousand dollar cash prize in addition to book publication.

For more information about either prize, visit **www.fencebooks.com**, or send an SASE to: Fence Books/[Name of Prize], 303 East Eighth Street, #B1, New York, New York, 10009.

For more about **FENCE**, visit **www.fencemag.com**.

FENCE BOOKS

The Alberta Prize

Practice, Restraint	Laura Sims
A Magic Book	Sasha Steensen
Sky Girl	Rosemary Griggs
The Real Moon of Poetry and Other Poems	Tina Celona
Zirconia	Chelsey Minnis

Fence Modern Poets Series

Povel	Geraldine Kim, selected by Forrest Gander
The Opening Question	Prageeta Sharma, selected by Peter Gizzi
Apprehend	Elizabeth Robinson, selected by Ann Lauterbach
The Red Bird	Joyelle McSweeney, selected by Allen Grossman

Free Choices

Folding Ruler Star	Aaron Kunin
The Commandrine and Other Poems	Joyelle McSweeney
Macular Hole	Catherine Wagner
Nota	Martin Corless-Smith
Father of Noise	Anthony McCann
Can You Relax in My House	Michael Earl Craig
Miss America	Catherine Wagner